GIANTS AND DEMONS

Ghatotkacha the Brave Giant

SHUBHA VILAS

Om KIDZ
An imprint of Om Books International

The mighty and strong Bhima met the demoness Hidimba when the Pandavas were living in the forest in exile. Bhima and Hidimba soon fell in love. Bhima's mother Kunti gave them permission to get married. Soon a son was born to them, who was half-human and half-demon. He was named Ghatotkacha.

The child got his name from the shape of his head which was round like a 'ghat', meaning 'clay pot' and 'utkach', meaning 'bald'. Ghatotkacha looked like a young adult as soon as he was born.

Ghatotkacha was a favourite of all his uncles, especially Yudhishthira. And also Krishna. Krishna had even given him a blessing that he would be the strongest man in the world.

Ghatotkacha was also blessed with magical powers. He could increase or decrease his size at will. When he increased his already enormous body, he could destroy any enemy.

Hidimba had promised Kunti that she would remain with Bhima only till the birth of a son. She soon realised that her stay with the Pandavas must end. So she went away, along with Ghatotkacha.

Ghatotkacha also took leave of his father and all other elders. Ghatotkacha loved his family as much as they loved him. He was always ready to serve them. He had given them a promise. He would appear before them whenever they needed his help. And it was a promise he kept all his life.

The Mahabharata was a deadly war between the Pandavas and their cousins, the Kauravas. The oldest Kaurava, Duryodhana, wanted to destroy the Pandavas. He had already tried to kill them many times. But they had always managed to escape safely. The war would now decide who would live, and who would die. Who would get the kingdom of Hastinapur? Who would get nothing?

The Kauravas had many expert warriors. The Pandavas desperately needed help. On the fourteenth day of the war, Krishna called Ghatotkacha to enter the scene. Ghatotkacha was their best warrior, given that he had many magical qualities. He was also much bigger in size. Killing Kauravas for him was like swatting mosquitoes.

Ghatotkacha started kicking all the chariots, horses and elephants. The arrows of the enemies were like toys for him. Fighting with people who were less than half his size was like fighting with children.

As the Kaurava soldiers started dying in large numbers, Duryodhana got worried. He was afraid that he would lose the war that very day itself. Not one person in his army could match the might of Ghatotkacha. He was not only a brave giant, he was also very strong.

Duryodhana began to think hard. Suddenly, he had an idea. He called his friend Karna. Now, Karna had a secret Shakti weapon that could be used only once. And he was planning to use that in his fight against his arch enemy, Arjuna. He wanted to kill Arjuna at any cost.

'Karna, I want you to use your most deadly weapon on Ghatotkacha,' Duryodhana pleaded.

'No, Duryodhana. I want to use it tomorrow on Arjuna,' Karna replied.

'But we will all die today, if you don't kill him now,' Duryodhana cried in desperation.

Forced by Duryodhana, Karna used his mighty weapon and killed Ghatotkacha. Even when Ghatotkacha fell, he killed millions of enemy soldiers by crushing them under his enormous weight. And not just that, he saved Arjuna from the Shakti weapon too. Ghatotkacha served the Pandavas even in death.